EXPLORING THE GREAT OUTDOORS

EXPLORING THE GREAT OUTDOORS

SERAPHINA WILDE

CONTENTS

1	Introduction to National Parks	1
2	History of National Parks	5
3	Geographical Diversity	7
4	Biodiversity and Conservation Efforts	11
5	Visitor Experience	15
6	Infrastructure and Facilities	19
7	Management and Administration	23
8	Challenges and Future Directions	27
9	Notable National Parks	29
10	Grand Canyon National Park	31
11	Yellowstone National Park	35
12	Acadia National Park	39
13	Everglades National Park	43
14	Conclusion and Reflections	47

Copyright © 2024 by Seraphina Wilde
All rights reserved. No part of this book may be reproduced in any manner whatsoever without written permission except in the case of brief quotations embodied in critical articles and reviews.
First Printing, 2024

CHAPTER 1

Introduction to National Parks

Before we can dive into the details of which park to visit, when, and for what purpose, we need to understand the meaning and significance of national parks as a whole. While some of us may have an excellent knowledge of the parks, others may know nothing about them beyond the fact that they involve nature. Understanding their function and purpose will help us to understand what specifically sets each park apart and what each offers the cautious traveler. Additionally, we will discuss the variety of landscapes in the United States that are represented in the park system, including the reason for their inclusion and an overview of their general features, throughout the remaining sections of this chapter.

National parks have been an essential part of the cultural, economic, and natural framework of the United States since their establishment in the late 19th and early 20th centuries. Often called the crown jewels of our country, the 60 national parks across the United States and its territories have been visited by millions and millions of people throughout the years. Whether they have visited in person or simply daydreamed about a trip, few fail to recognize the significance of these areas to the nation as a whole. Just as importantly, these parks offer something unique and essential to their guests. In this book, we will explore the ins and outs of the national parks; the how, the where, the why, and the history of each individual area from the most visited to the most remote and unknown to the modern traveler.

Definition and Significance of National Parks

From individual parks to entire countries, the world has worked to preserve the natural beauty and cultural heritage of many locations around the world. As one such way to accomplish this goal, the United States of America, one of the countries to adopt the idea of national parks, now boasts more than sixty national parks that span the American landscape. One might ask, however, what constitutes a national park? Why are these unique places valuable? The purpose of this subsection will be to explore the concept of a national park itself. In the subsections to follow, relevant questions will be answered about this unique group of natural areas, why they were set apart, and what the people of America have deemed worth preserving.

In 1916, when the Department of the Interior was brand new, President Woodrow Wilson signed what would become the National Park Service into law. What, though, was the reason behind doing so? President Wilson states, "The fundamental idea of the national parks...is that the country belongs to the people, that it is in process of making for the enrichment of the lives of all of us." To translate, the concept of a national park is to ensure that people always have places that are cared for and reserved specifically for them, and that the places in question are valuable precisely because they remain unblemished by human influence. Furthermore, President Wilson goes on to state that besides their vast natural beauty, the national parks were to be set aside and recognized as valuable for their representation of the nation's history. Such a neat definition can be summarized, then, that national parks exist to preserve for posterity a country's landscapes and heritage exactly as they were before.

CHAPTER 2

History of National Parks

1872: On March 1, President Ulysses S. Grant signs a bill declaring the Yellowstone region in Wyoming and Montana as a public pleasure ground. Although this park was public, and thus different than a state park, there was no system for management, so it was not effectively administered.

1890: President Benjamin Harrison signs a law that creates the nation's first forest reserve (later the national forest). Gifford Pinchot, a pioneer in the conservation movement, was entrusted with the task of managing these forests in a way that would provide for their protection as well as the extraction of resources.

1903: John Muir visits Yosemite Valley and presents a 3-page document to President Theodore Roosevelt. In it, Muir encourages the President to return the park's control to the federal government to prevent its continued commercialization.

1906: Congress passes the Antiquities Act, granting the President discretion to create national monuments from public lands in order to preserve for posterity "objects of historic or scientific interest". This act was largely designed to allow for the protection of archaeological sites on the U.S. mainland and in the newly acquired territories that did not enjoy park or forest status.

1916: The National Park Service is created to manage the national parks and monuments now overseen by the U.S. Department of the Interior. The Organic Act was authorized by Congress and established an agency within the Department of the Interior responsible for the care of 35 national parks, monuments, and reservations previously managed by the Department's General Land Office as well as any future national parks.

Key Events and Legislation

National parks are natural treasures that the world has been exploring and enjoying since Yellowstone National Park was established in 1872. This section offers a detail of key events and significant legislative actions pertaining to the national parks and the systems that help manage the operation and rehabilitation of our national park units. Subsequent sections focus on the beginning of the national park idea, which highlights why the national parks are so essential to the American public. A more extensive list of key events in the national parks can be found in Table 1.2. During his last days in office, President Ulysses S. Grant signed into law a bill that for the first time set aside public lands, approximately two million acres, 'as a public park and pleasure ground for the benefit and enjoyment of the people.' The Act of 1872, establishing Yellowstone National Park, not only created the world's first national park, but it also established a model for what is now referred to as the National Park System. Other milestones that mark significant events and actions in the development of national parks were accomplished years after the creation of Yellowstone, which, as will be described in the following section, was a deviation from the original "idea of a park." This early action focused only on the setting aside of public land and did not address how the park would be managed or rehabilitated.

CHAPTER 3

Geographical Diversity

Come journey with us as we explore the many national parks in the United States! In "America's Best Idea," also known as the National Park Service, the United States Congress presides over 58 national parks and over 10,000 National Register of Historic Places sites, including over 400 national parks that preserve a wide variety of special places, from natural icons to historic sites. These 58 national parks can be found dispersed throughout the entire United States. From the East to the West coast, these parks shed light on the natural bounty of the many lands that make up our country, demonstrate their unique and specialized ecosystems, and replay the stories told with rocks and plants and animals found in each.

Geographical Diversity Did you know that the national parks of the United States contain 75,000 archaeological sites, including 26,000 prehistoric structures, built by Native Americans? These locations represent the diversity of Native American cultural landscapes and the historical convergence of tribal interests and environmental activities. Apart from the ancient structures humans have left behind in the parks, the parks themselves, freckled across the United States, create dazzling landscapes, each vastly different than the last. In America, there are parklands that are structurally meadows, deserts, alpines, estuaries, hydrologic systems, glades, island seascapes, dry forest, freshwater systems, swamp bottoms, dunes, alvars, mineral outcrops, river systems, sandstone, and bogs. The parks house the highest mountains on every continent, lowest depressions on every sea, and the tallest trees in the world! Did you know that parks in the contiguous 48 states depict regions which cover only 18% of the United States, yet are home to 63% of America's known plant species and 50% of the known vertebrate species? The national parks also preserve the few remaining undisturbed ecosystems that were present when Europeans arrived in America and contain the most significant examples of major biotic and environmental events of the last two million years.

Different Types of Landscapes Found in National Parks

National parks in the United States are some of the most varied and uniquely beautiful places in the country. They spread over various geological regions from the volcanic islands of Hawai'i to the meadows of Florida, and encompass everything from high desert to sub-alpine forests and coral reefs. The majority of these parks, however, were designated to preserve instances of a specific landscape, many of them notable for their size, natural beauty, and the immensity of the processes responsible for creating them. It can be useful to think about this in terms of the paintings of a specific landscape, and while each landscape itself is unique, it can also be subdivided into categories based on similar features.

Erosional landscapes are some of the most common in the National Park Service, and are characterized by the action of rivers, glaciers, and wind in carving away at the bedrock beneath them. They include deep canyons, sharp spires, and sculpted sandstone formations. Lava and ash fields are made up almost entirely of igneous rock from volcanic sources, creating pahoehoe and a'a lava, cinder cones, and perhaps even entire geothermal basins. Glacial landscapes show the wear of the expansion and retreat of alpine ice fields, most commonly leaving behind in its wake horn peaks, aretes, cirques and tarns, as well as offering the occasional iceberg-filled lake. Far less common are coastal landscapes that vary wildly from stark cliffs to golden sands and mangrove forests. Lastly, there are the monumental geologic features and mountain ranges that stretch from California to Maine, their form steeped in their tectonic histories.

CHAPTER 4

Biodiversity and Conservation Efforts

Boasting an extraordinary collection of landscapes, from mountains to desert, national parks are homes to thousands of species of flora and fauna. In terms of vertebrates, a grand total of 840 can be found in the 63 national parks spread over 730,000 square miles. The range of flora is even more impressive, with over 3,800 species of plant across only 60 of the parks. This staggering biodiversity is supported by the parks' ability to preserve habitats. Terrestrial and aquatic ecosystems including old-growth forests, coral atolls, and even deep interiors of caves are represented, making them important topics for ecological research - and there's much to study, with the recorded number of species of plants, insects, fungi and arachnids in the national parks at approximately 17,000. And that is far from the actual number of species, considering that in the United States alone, an estimated over 12,000 new species of insects are discovered each year.

This huge variety of flora and fauna supports the overall concept of ecosystem function and service. Every national park contains tens of different ecosystems. And crucially, the beauty of the national parks and their moving landscapes allow humans to experience what biologist E. O. Wilson termed biophilia, our innately emotional affiliation with other living organisms. In fact, biologist Roger Ulrich stated that vivid natural scenes trigger feelings of wonder and even spirituality. Thus, preserved miles of the national parks contribute to the well-being of most of the people, both consciously and unconsciously. In essence, the national parks are a reserve of unlimited potential for all societal groups. The future benefits of wildlife for those large groups of future people, however, are at the mercy of our contemporary decisions. Therefore, we must protect and foster the splendor of the national parks.

Flora and Fauna in National Parks
National Park Flora and Fauna
In addition to awe-inspiring natural landscapes, national parks are also home to an incredible diversity of plant and animal species. According to the National Park Service, there are more than 5,000 plant species, over 200 mammal species, and around 800 bird species spread among the national parks. An additional 300 reptile and amphibian species, 250 fish species, and an astounding 25,000 insect species are also an integral part of these ecosystems. With such wide-ranging biodiversity contained within national park borders, it is easy to see the biological significance these protected areas have within the larger frame of the natural world. It is also easy to see why preservation and conservation measures are necessary in order to protect the integrity of these diverse and complex ecosystems.

Within ecosystems, plants are considered producers because they create their own food using various inorganic compounds in the presence of sunlight. This self-conversion of energy is called photosynthesis. Mammals, including many that are often associated with the Old West, are also residents in some of the national parks. These large animals include elk, deer, buffalo, and bears in parks such as

Yellowstone, Glacier, and Zion, which were once roamed the western landscape nearly uninhibited. As with plants, carnivorous predators are also residents of some parks and hold important positions in the food chain. Other animals that roam the expansive grasslands and forests of this park network include little critters such as squirrels, rabbits, and chipmunks. This diverse combination of species both large and small contribute to the ecological balances of their unique habitat areas.

CHAPTER 5

Visitor Experience

National parks are primarily destinations for park visitors seeking recreational opportunities, although the educational benefits of those visits should not be minimized. There are many types of visitor experiences available in the park system, and national parks are particularly known for their natural scenic beauty. Below is a list of some of what visitors can do in national parks:

1. Recreate - Hike - Kayak - Canoe - Fish - Boat - Horseback ride - Off-road vehicle - Ride a bicycle - Jog - Mountain climb - Hunt - Sight-see - Photograph

2. Special Use Permits - Camping (campfire, picnic) - Backpacking (permit, campfire, sanitation) - Hunting (permit) - Commercial photography (permit)

3. Interact with the Environment - Camp - Fish - Build a campfire - Picnic - Take photographs - Watch wildlife - Engage in bird watching - Stargaze

4. Special Programs - Ranger-led hikes - Campfire programs - Thematic evenings - Interpretive walks - Visits to cultural demonstrations - Lectures/seminars

While there are a myriad of ways to find enjoyment in the national parks across the United States, prospective visitors will want to choose their park destination based on what places offer them the types of experiences they may be seeking. From a desire for adventure to enlightenment, these natural wonders of the U.S. inspire both the young and old with new experiences and a yearning to explore what lies just beyond the next valley or mountaintop.

Recreational Activities Available in National Parks

In addition to providing information on individual national parks, readers will find extensive information about recreational activities. Operating under the National Park Service, the primary objectives of the National Park System are to conserve natural and cultural resources and to protect national parks while still allowing individuals to experience and enjoy those places. There is a strong emphasis on outdoor activities in most national parks. National parks are home to a wide range of outdoor activities and cater to a wide range of interests, including activities that facilitate wilderness experiences, like hiking and rock climbing. Camping, cycling, and endless water-based activities attract individuals of all ages and are common in national parks with accessible waterways. It is possible to fly to locations inhabited by a limited selection of national birds and animals.

In most urban national parks, including those in towns (urban recreation areas, which receive millions of visitors annually), there are recreational opportunities such as city walks, held sporting events, viewing wildlife, guided tours, and numerous other, often historically or culturally oriented events. Campfires, barbecues, and fireworks may be included in recreational activities, depending on the recreation and time of year, and where within a national park they are pursued. The America the Beautiful pass is an affordable way to access national parks and perform numerous low-priced recreational activities in safe, well-protected areas, and at a reasonable expense. The sports and other physical activity undertaken in national parks can be detrimental to health, mainly when undertaken in unusual surroundings, without the knowledge of individual park trails.

CHAPTER 6

Infrastructure and Facilities

Visitors can expect to find various facilities and infrastructure within these protected areas. The National Park Service is mandated to ensure park facilities and infrastructure are properly maintained and are in their best form possible. The intention of the National Park Service is to ensure facilities and infrastructure preserve the vast natural resources that parks represent while ensuring visitor comfort and access. All facilities, including bathrooms and lodges, are operated under strict recycling and energy initiatives at a park-specific level. Park rangers, entrance gates, and law enforcement officials work to ensure that guests are safe and comfortable throughout their visits.

The National Park Service is known to focus on public-use facilities and visitor safety. With such a heavy mobile population in the United States, the National Park Service ensures parking and remarkable roadways are in their best shape. A lot of different roads run through the national parks and have often been designated as National Scenic Byways. This is done to ensure public access and safety, as the National Scenic Byways program ensures traveling routes throughout the United States are especially noteworthy and revered as routes spread across landscapes and cultural affluence. Most visitors to national parks will find food, lodging, camping, educational, and guiding services right there at the National Park Service facilities. National parks do range in their amenities but all provide visitor comfort and knowledge. National Park Service Information Centers are largely the best places to acquire personalized park information. Each national park campground is also maintained by the National Park Service. These campgrounds provide picnic tables, fire pits, and paved site parking. Some National Parks offer laundry, showers, and restaurants in their campgrounds; certain campsites must be reserved in advance while others are issued on a first-come, first-serve basis.

Accommodation Options and Visitor Centers

Accommodation options in the national parks include campsites, lodges, and hotels. One in five campsites can be booked ahead of time on the official National Park website, and most national parks offer first-come-first-served sites that are not reservable in advance. Visitors should check the specific park page to find out how camping works at that specific park. Lodges and hotels are also owned by private companies and require an advanced reservation. Each park has a visitor center with rangers and volunteers who can answer questions, help plan out a visit, and provide maps and brochures. For additional resources, visit the official website, place a call to the park, or mail a letter.

Each visitor center can provide a different view of the parks, and the various rangers are always more than happy to answer any questions or provide advice based on their experiences. Aside from the visitor centers, the trails and various points of interest inside the national park itself are excellent places to view nature and wildlife. The smaller the trail, the more untouched and unspoiled the experience can be. Try to visit these places early in the morning or during wildlife feeding hours. Lastly, most national parks are good for casual viewing when driving through the park, as all of the roads are designated scenic by the respective states.

CHAPTER 7

Management and Administration

Management and Administration: This section goes into the bureaucratic details of how this fifth of the book actually plays out. It is administrative more than casual reading, but may be of interest to those who are curious about such things. National Parks are meant to be managed so that their resources are enjoyed in a balanced way by this and future generations, and the following section describes what organizations are in charge.

In the United States, management of all currently existing national parks and national monuments is the responsibility of the National Park Service, an agency of the Department of the Interior. These areas were brought together from several different agencies when the Park Service was created in 1916. The function of the National Park Service is to conserve the scenery, the natural and historic objects, and the wildlife in the parks, but also to provide for the enjoyment of these parks in a way that will leave these assets "unimpaired for the enjoyment of future generations". Concern about the national parks showed such a decline by the 1980s that a massive reorganization took place to try and prevent this, supported by the Department of the Interior, Congress, and a committee headed by

Lloyd N. Cutler. This involved a standardization of operational procedures and unit identification, as well as more institutionalized congressional support. Besides the National Park Service itself, other organizations like the National Park Foundation, an official nonprofit association, are also involved in keeping the parks suitable for interested tourists.

Role of the National Park Service

The National Park Service is the entity within the U.S. Department of the Interior responsible for upholding and maintaining national parks. It is also tasked with providing a gateway to nature and explaining in detail the purpose, geology, botany, zoology, history, culture, language, art, and architecture of the park. To maintain and control human impacts, the NPS's primary mission is to guard the park's wealth. They must also have an elected director known as the Director of the United States National Park Service. Many of the people in the agency are law enforcement officers who patrol parks to ensure that the wildlife, land, and links are used in accordance with existing legislation. Those who break laws are usually sentenced to a significant amount of jail time. Campgrounds, and in some situations, hotels, restaurants, nature shops, or other institutions, are used to provide housing to tourists.

The National Park Service (NPS) is the federal government agency that oversees and preserves the national parks of the United States of America. Prior to the formation of the NPS, reservations had been taken care of by the U.S. Army, and park officers had been held in this way. At first, National Monuments have been commissioned to the United States Department of War in conjunction with the Land Service's remit and have been supervised by the U.S. militia. The communities, whose persecution caused the conviction that the U.S. Army not had the military commitment or governmental clout to account for the qualifications, were trying to minimize and disliked auctioning some of the biggest fauna in the community. The Hetch Hetchy settlement, which persuaded anyone who appreciated regulation and that a solitary control system was required, persuaded Congress to establish a separate State Ministry.

CHAPTER 8

Challenges and Future Directions

Despite their established legal designations and years of advocacy on their behalf, the national parks remain vulnerable to threats that also menace the rest of the world's ecosystems. Whether they come from outside the parks—emerging markets in Asia are now fueling a trade in rare species of plants and animals that is quickly decimating populations in Africa and Southeast Asia, for example—or are generated by the markets and populations of the United States itself, such as pollution and climate change. All of which threaten species and habitats that do not respect the boundaries of the national parks, will require a recommitment by the people of the United States to protect nature.

Flames are not the only agents of change in natural areas protected for their scenic beauty, wildlife, and other resources; the National Park Service has been charged with trying to eliminate many such insults, and today all national parks and most other areas managed by the agency are mandated to preserve the ecosystems. The park service's new ecosystem-management initiatives, including the development of "biosphere reserves" identified "by, for, and with the people" in parks and surrounding communities, are hopeful, indeed visionary signs that the dual paradoxes of preservation in a sea of change and changeability and "management" in a loss of parks are beginning to be boldly addressed.

Environmental Threats and Sustainability Measures
Introduction to the United States' National Parks
Environmental Threats: As havens in our increasingly developed world, national parks face many environmental threats. While they have always been this way, the challenges of the 21st century are not only the usual "stable" environmental problems associated with climate change, however. Each new administration has the potential to bring a completely new host of plans for fossil fuel extraction, mining, and logging into the national park system. Environmental issues can affect almost any aspect of life-forms, like weather catastrophes and their effects on the Earth's plateaus, which are difficult to foresee and predict. This, in turn, raises questions about whether the preservation of national parks is a more substantial and adequate option, how much it expenditures to conserve them, and what that forgiveness would look like.

Sustainability Sustainability is a combination of long-term environmental protection and the idea that it is also quite likely for human civilizations and businesses to be in competitive dominance for generations. Many of today's well-managed parks are attempting to manage their practices in a sustainable manner, such as utilizing better transit options rather than private cars, and electricity in buildings is sometimes generated by solar power. Sustaining parks necessitates further interest and more subtle consideration. Parks are flourishing, and they are making every effort to make sure it stays that way to ensure they are an everlasting attribute of the United States.

CHAPTER 9

Notable National Parks

Acadia National Park • This is the only national park in the state of Maine, known for its beautiful coastline and vibrant forests. • A picture of tranquility, the park offers many opportunities for paddling, sailing, and scenic drives. • Visitors can climb the highest peak on the Atlantic coast (Cadillac Mountain) or visit the only fjord on the East Coast (Sommes Sound).

Zion National Park • Zion National Park is Utah's first national park. • The land is a maze of buttes, canyons, mesas, and amazing beauty. • People come from all around the world to experience the Riverside Walk and to hike the Chain section of Angel's Landing. • $2 million was spent on today's equivalent of nearly 100 miles of what is known as Mount Carmel Highway. A tunnel was even blasted through the rock so that the road would be more easily passable.

Yellowstone National Park • Fondly known as "the granddaddy of the national parks," Yellowstone National Park was where the idea of the national park was born. • Established in 1872, this Wyoming park is known for its granddaddy-sized attractions: the largest concentration of geysers in the world, an impressive population of grizzly and black bears, and the park's mammoth-sized, namesake caldera.

Arches National Park • Located just outside of Moab, Utah, Arches National Park is home to more than 2,000 natural arches, including the most famous one: Delicate Arch. • The Windows, Double Arch, Landscape Arch, and The Devil's Garden are also notable attractions within the park.

Yosemite National Park
Designated: 1890 Size: 1,169 square miles Highlight: Tunnel View

Although Yosemite is not one of the largest national parks in the United States, it's one of the most visited. That title comes as no surprise when you learn of the valley's immense grandeur. All around, steep granite cliffs form enormous faces like El Capitan and Half Dome, two of the most famous rock formations on Planet Earth. The iconic Tunnel View, just as you enter the park portal, is arguably the most beloved photo op along the entire Route 1. The view from Inspiration Point, just another tower up, is guaranteed to inspire.

One of my favorite things about Yosemite that distinguishes it from the rest of the national parks is its 800 miles of hiking trails and roads. Sure, there are some heavy hitters out there, but the park claims some of the most pristine and diverse ecosystems in North America. Ranging from arid desert to snowy alpine, each zone has its own beautiful plants and animals to find, and the stunning geographic features are bound to capture your attention. Head over to the official website for adventure planning help and more hidden gems to explore. Note that some remote areas require permits to enter, so make sure to plan ahead.

CHAPTER 10

Grand Canyon National Park

Desert View Region; Yavapai Point; Duck on a Rock; Mule Ride; AAVIP/ Below the Rim; Canyon Visitor Cafe; Tusayan Ruins; Mary Colter designed buildings; Navajo's; Douglas fuming at edge of canyon.

The breathtaking sight of the Grand Canyon has long been known as one of the wonders of the world, but its importance transcends the ability of the landscape to open human mouths. As the scenic centerpiece of the Grand Canyon Unit, Grand Canyon National Park remains one of the great "halls of fame": citizens from around the world traverse the globe to walk the park's high walkways and ride an ancient river draw. They come not only to admire the canyon but, through their admiration, to partake in a festive, almost sacramental American experience. The winning of the west, manifest destiny, man against nature, landscape as a metaphor for the sublime—all of these themes loom large in the visitor's mind.

Grand Canyon National Park is 1 in 58 areas protected by the NPS. This places the park in the very first year of designation when there is 1 class standing for every year of national park history. The Grand Canyon first came to the attention of the scientific community in 1855, when Lt. Joseph C. Ives, sent by the U.S. Army for the purpose of surveying the Colorado River between the Virgin and Bill Williams forks, proclaimed that the Grand Canyon was "altogether valueless" and the river "can be of no possible use to the public." Today, the Colorado River is "public stock," providing water to over 35 million people, and the Grand Canyon is a cornerstone of one of the grandest scientific institutions in the world—the National Park Service.

Historical Significance and Geological Features
The Grand Canyon National Park overlaps the borders of both the state of Arizona and the Hualapai Reservation. It is home to one of the most iconic landscapes found in the southwest region of the United States, attracting millions of visitors to its rim each year. This immense canyon was deeply carved by the Colorado River over the course of many millennia as it flowed downstream. Erosional forces have since unveiled over 40 distinct rock layers that now span a whopping 1.75 to 2 billion years of Earth's history, shaping the gorges and fascinating formations that we identify with this park today. Here, it is also possible to explore evidence left behind by extraterrestrial life as well as take a stroll along ancient eroded beaches left behind by a long-gone ocean.

The Grand Canyon National Park is such a treasure because of the unique history that is recorded in the many layers of rock and sediment here. This canyon stands unrivaled either in the United States or any other part of the world for its immense depth and enormous expansiveness that works tremendously well to preserve over three quarters of the sedimentary time. Geological investigations are usually awarded a global renown to the park's history owing to its immense size, depth, and its linear and nearly ideal uplift that leaves it at an elevation between 2000-9000 feet above sea level. This body of work has been built on a foundation that relies on a tremendous amount of detailed field observations and comparisons from across the globe, allowing it to gradually become influential in how geologists from all backgrounds interpret hogbacks, monoclines, and basins in non-marine sedimentary environments.

CHAPTER 11

Yellowstone National Park

A visit to the United States and its national parks cannot possibly offer you a complete experience of its wild, rugged beauty without first stopping by Yellowstone National Park, the oldest and one of the most beloved nature reserves in North America. This large American national park is primarily situated in the state of Wyoming and crosses over into Idaho and Montana. Yellowstone covers a vast expanse of wilderness and is home to a wide variety of ecosystems, including alpine, subalpine, and valley systems. It covers more than two million acres and is centered on the famous Yellowstone Caldera, the largest supervolcano on the continent.

While that alone is a pretty interesting fact, Yellowstone National Park has an impressive history of interesting natural spectacles and events. It embraces an active geothermal area with breathtaking hot springs, mud pools, geysers, and fumaroles, creating a true otherworldly atmosphere. Yellowstone's main claim to fame is that it was the first national park to ever be built in the world and was effectively the birthplace of the United States National Parks System. In addition, the park is home to a myriad of important wildlife species, many of which were driven to the brink of extinction before they were reintroduced to the Yellowstone area. Many of these species are now healthy in this area and maintained in good numbers. Among others, the large mammals that you can potentially spot include bison, grizzly bears, elk, moose, and wolves.

Geothermal Features and Wildlife

Geothermal Features Each year, more than 11,000 hydrothermal features erupt in Yellowstone, releasing more than 3,300 tons of various compounds. The most popular place to see geothermal features is the Lower Loop of the Grand Loop, which is the world's greatest concentration of geysers. The most famous feature is Old Faithful Geyser, which erupts at an almost precise interval of about every 90 minutes to a height of 100 to 180 feet for about one minute. Most eruptions are about 130 feet. The Upper Loop also has several features perfect for viewing, such as the Midway Geyser Basin that contains Grand Prismatic Spring, Jumping Rainbow, and Excelsior geysers. The Lower Geyser Basin contains mid- to low-steaming geysers and fumaroles. About 98 percent of the world's geysers are in the United States, and most are found in Yellowstone.

Wildlife About 67 mammals live here, including grizzly and black bears, lynx, wolverine, badgers, marten, otter, mountain lions, bats, elk, bison, mountain goats, bighorn sheep, moose, mule and whitetail deer, and the extremely rare woodland caribou. The bison herd is the oldest and largest in the United States, and elk are found in the greatest concentration. In winter, visitors can observe both bison and elk. Coyotes and wolves also inhabit the park. More than 300 species of birds live in, migrate to, or travel through Yellowstone. Bear species include the black bear and the grizzly bear. Black bears can weigh up to 250 pounds, while grizzly bears can weigh up to 800 pounds. Grizzly bears are also much more aggressive than black bears. Visitors should carry pepper spray when hiking or walking in the backcountry, and cars should be equipped with air horns or other noisemakers in bear country.

CHAPTER 12

Acadia National Park

Dominated by coastal landscapes, it was Arno B. Cammerer who persuaded Congress that the forests and stony shores of Mount Desert Island lay in one of the few places appropriate for making improvements for a national park of distinctive character. Established as Sieur de Monts National Monument in 1916, it became, three years later, the first instance where the private sector donated funds to purchase land for a national park. George B. Dorr was the motivating force of the Hancock County Trustees of Public Reservations, successor to the original Sieur de Mont Nature Preserve. The lands in Boston's "Swiss Chalet" and "Wild Gardens of Acadia" later acquired the lands in trust. In 1929, along with Sugarloaf Mountain, the nearly 1,500-foot (457-m) Schoodic Peninsula became part of the park, while Isle au Haut, with an average of 515 feet (157 m) in elevation, was added in 1931. Most of the area was ravaged by the Oct. 17, 1947, fire, but forest communities have largely reestablished themselves.

LENGTH: Exploring the park may take 2-7 days, depending on how much you want to hike, bike, swim, fish, and boat. For a quick visit, figure on 2 days. For a leisurely, in-depth experience, set aside 3-4 days. The park's activities allow for spending up to 7 days in the area including Mount Desert Island, the Schoodic Peninsula, and Castine. ACCESS: The closest publicly accessible commercial air service is located in Bangor, Maine. The park is less than a 1-hour drive from the city. BY GROUND: Interstate 95 brings travelers from the south and north directly to Bangor, Maine, while the scenic coastal route, U.S. Route 1, also connects with Bangor in Calais, Maine. From Bangor, take U.S. 1A and 3 to Ellsworth. Continue on Maine Route 3 to Mount Desert Island and Schoodic Peninsula. OFFICIAL VISITOR CENTERS: Significant park road logs begin here, ranging from WWI automobile trips to guidebooks of the 1960s. ENTRANCE FEES: Now waived by the federal government for all visitors.

Coastal Landscapes and Activities
Coastal landscapes and activities. What makes Acadia truly outside of the ordinary is the way those landscapes and experiences tie the park to the coast.

Island jewels: Both the Schoodic Peninsula and Mount Desert Island offer some of the coolest geological specimens you'll find on the coast.

Lowdown: Nearly a quarter of park visitation happens at Sand Beach, the only oceanfront beach in the park! Average water temperatures exceed 55 degrees from June into the fall, but aren't swimming temperature until at least late June. The natural inlet between Thunder Hole and Sand Beach sometimes cuts off access between them during especially high tides and/or stormy conditions. Schoodic was only recently designated Acadia National Park. Before being taken under the NPS wing, it was operated as the Schoodic District of Acadia NP although separated from the main body of the park by Frenchman Bay and accessible only by ferry. The park included the 26,770-acre peninsula and 13,636 offshore acres. Viking Lumber Company sold the land to the federal government for $1 plus land interests when it ceased commercial operations on September 3, 1929. The historic Naval listening station at Schoodic Head continued to operate on a two-acre leased U.S. Navy parcel until 2002. The Schoodic Mountains consist of mountains in the central and southeastern part of the park. To the west, the mountains rise steeply from the 190-acre park. The mountains do not overlook Frenchman Bay and are not wholly visible from the ocean drive on Mount Desert Island.

CHAPTER 13

Everglades National Park

Ecosystem: Everglades National Park was established to save a unique example of the original flora and fauna that once characterized South Florida. Its charming birds, strange reptiles and insects, magnificently rich vegetation, and seemingly endless miles of fresh and brackish water make this, the largest of the United States National Parks, almost a tropical paradise right at the nation's door. A distinctive feature of the Everglades, which is popularly believed to cover the entire park, is a vast plain of slow-moving water, averaging only six inches in depth, with occasional streamers visible winding their way through dense sawgrass over the entire countryside. Yet the park carefully avoids areas of indefinite value to bring within its boundaries the richest variety of wildlife and most complete array of jungle types to be found in the wilderness.

Pioneers: Historically, the Everglades was a natural home for the Seminole and Miccosukee Indians, and afterwards there occurred several large pioneer establishments in the 1800s and early 1900s: Chokoloskee, Royal Palm, Fort Dallas, and the now-abandoned Flamingo. The town of Homestead, too, was established in an area now included by the park. Most of these developmental activities, however, failed partly because of the demands of the minute and immensely complicated hydrology required for successful sugar and rice planting, and due in part to the subsequent decline in the prices of these crops. People found it impossible to farm the swamp. The future potential for economic vegetation development is mainly for such decorative tropicals as Calathea and Adromischus for trial employment of the newer building block materials such as sugarcane-bagasse insulation, and in nonagricultural absorption by acritax club members of the beauty of the Everglades.

Management/Protection: Everglades National Park is composed of lands and waters needed to preserve a portion of the world-famous Everglades. The objective of said park is to preserve and protect from despoliation the unique fauna and flora of the area, the tender grass-wood junctures, the contrasting hammocks, as well as the sea, bay, and upland bird short-grass abodes.

Unique Ecosystems and Conservation Efforts

The park's unique ecosystems support 12 distinct habitats, ranging from coastal mangrove and island systems to pine woods and sawgrass prairies situated on freshwater prairies in the backcountry. The subtropical climates of the Everglades are responsible for the park's abundance of floral species—there are over 1,000 plants native to the region. Representatives from other animal groups in the Everglades include crucial nesting grounds for several species of wading birds and marine birds, including tern, heron, and roseate spoonbills. Marine bird populations surge throughout wintertime due to migration. In some cases, some 34 species have been reported within the park. The mangroves are the only place on the planet where both American crocodiles and alligators interact in this kind of environment. Globally endangered American crocodiles—just around 2000 were estimated in the wild throughout the year 2003 (approximately 500 at Cape Sable)—inhabit salty coastal oceans and bodies of freshwater, whereas American alligators inhabit only freshwater bodies of water.

The national park was open to the public from 1933 onwards. Scotts Hammock, Royal Palm, and Parsons Slough were owned by developers in the 1920s and 1930s, and these areas later became part of the original natural preserve. These areas were acquired from Colliers, a wealthy advertising client, and his executive friends, who saw the preserve's possibility. The national park declared 13,000 acres of parkland on May 30, 1934, ready to plan. The controversial proposed park expansion, which was proposed in 1947, lasted many years and involved considerable debate between environmentalists, developers, and would-be private property owners. The park now includes 1,399 million acres, including the first 1,100 square miles. The park retains its character as a result of land growth. Expanding the southern reach of the stream lowers salinity levels and raises freshened water supplies to encourage saltwater-conditioned plants suitable for birds and flora. In 1928, legal guardians told Colliers about natural preservation plans. In 1947, Everglades fought to expand the park for sale, even though rumors spread about an impending squander that the planning commission's existing commissioners indicated. However, a few years had led the legislature not to abandon the survey. Judicial opportunities were said to have the measure on proof and jail time. Since 1968, publicly controversial various proposals, involving the plan, development, and direction of the national park, were involved by public groups, tied to the plan, that were integrated into the framework of industrial development. United proposals have been put forward for precautions and conservation about other uses, especially Everglades National Park.

CHAPTER 14

Conclusion and Reflections

The impact on society. The national park idea is primarily aimed at individuals rather than at society. It offers the opportunity to become familiar with remote and unique undeveloped areas that have remained essentially so since the creation of the East African Game Preserve around the castle ruins of King Edward V of England in 1897. By the mid-twentieth century, all the horizons may have motor roads, but the land the hiker finds will have been little affected by thoughtless use. When mature, we think our system of national parks will have an ever-increasing value, as shown in the present case of Yellowstone Park.

The people they attract shall contribute their part to the emotional life around them. This is shipped from below, but from above, the national parks will always continue to be islands of peace where people can find something far away from mankind. This trapper told me about the freedom of the life lived by the hikers and people who traveled by, to see the world that Hemingway wrote about. Would not sooner or later gas stations, a flying field, and summer homes ruin the waxing, the real, and the road, the national parks? The fundamental thought of the National Park Service is that, whoever they are, there will always be an increasing number of people who will be akin to the ideal who shall, while on this earth, enjoy the supreme experience of living for a few days in the vast solitude and wilderness of the wilderness mantle. In reality, the national parks began, in fact, with a series of treaty-guaranteed religious freedoms, by the discovery and acquisition of millions of acres of small, safe, and secure – if small – towns, after the death army of "disharmony" and "rivalry" – at the westward sweeping banded city.

Impact of National Parks on Society and Future Generations
Society and Future Generations

National parks have become a prominent aspect of our society and culture with a major impact on the American citizen. By driving across town into a park, spending a family vacation in the rugged backwoods, or gazing at a protected landscape from a passing airplane, millions of Americans have either directly or indirectly become associated with the national park system. They have come to realize and develop a sense of pride and ownership in the national park system because national parks are the tangible symbols of America's national heritage and natural treasures, and provide numerous social, cultural, and environmental values and services. National parks not only make a nation wealthy in culture and environment but also facilitate proper growth in respect to economic development and societal norms.

National parks are at the foundation of the topographical and emotional lebensraum of society and also national identity. The beats, Serpa, and seats of higher learning have precisely affected the emotional lebensraum of native individuals and international vacationers by college foster association with wildlands. The New World kids still feel an association with natural instruments in the New World. The natural world in the US land of opportunity not only fosters and shapes society's values and aspirations but also compels current and future generations to communicate directives engaging a huge range of environmental problems. I realize the worth of Yosemite Park or the park system to society and believe these natural instruments have to be saved because I want to live in my house there.

www.ingramcontent.com/pod-product-compliance
Lightning Source LLC
LaVergne TN
LVHW092059060526
838201LV00047B/1475